M000082230

This Book Belongs To

....

BRIGHT SPOTS
JOURNAL

CHRONICLE BOOKS
San Francisco

ISBN 978-1-4521-2933-4

Manufactured in China

MIX
Paper from
responsible sources
FSC® C016973

Designed by Allison Weiner

10 9 8 7 6 5 4 3 2

Chronicle Books LLC
680 Second Street
San Francisco, California 94107
www.chroniclebooks.com

HOW TO USE THIS BOOK

The best part of your day is always worth remembering! This journal is a place for you to record the bright spots in your life. A sunny weekend morning. The perfect cup of coffee enjoyed in bed. A good deal on a great pair of shoes. A long conversation with a close friend. Soon you'll have a collection of life's sweetest moments and will cultivate the habit of recognizing and appreciating all the little things that brighten your days.

date _____

date _____

date _____

. . . .

date _____

date _____

date _____

date _____

date _____

date _____

date _____

date _____

....

date _____

date _____

. . . .

date _____

date _____

date _____

date _____

date _____

date _____

date _____

date _____

- -

date _____